THE PARSON ON DANCING.

THE PARSON

ON

DANCING

AS IT IS TAUGHT IN THE BIBLE, AND WAS PRACTICED
AMONG THE ANCIENT GREEKS AND ROMANS.

BY

REV. J. B. GROSS,

AUTHOR OF THE HEATHEN RELIGION IN ITS POPULAR AND SYMBOLICAL
DEVELOPMENT; OF THE DOCTRINE OF THE LORD'S SUPPER AS SET
FORTH IN THE BOOK OF CONCORD, CRITICALLY EXAMINED AND
ITS FALLACY DEMONSTRATED; OF THE TEACHINGS OF PROVI-
DENCE, OR NEW LESSONS ON OLD SUBJECTS, &C.

Pleasure's the only noble end,
To which all human powers should tend;
And virtue gives her heavenly lore
But to make pleasure please us more.—MOORE.

There is no sterner moralist than pleasure.—BYRON.

DANCE HORIZONS · NEW YORK

One of a series of republications by Dance Horizons, 1801 East 26th Street, Brooklyn, N.Y. 11229

This is an unabridged republication of the first edition published by J. B. Lippincott & Co., Philadelphia, in 1879.

International Standard Book Number 0-87127-079-X

Library of Congress Catalog Card Number 75-9163

Printed in the United States of America

DEDICATION.

To the patrons of *the Dance*, whose Conduct is guided by Seemliness and Discretion—the enlightened Friends of an Innocent and Healthful Pastime, who wisely seek to combine Recreation with Toil, and thus alleviate some of the Many Cares as well as to bear with More Facility and Cheerfulness the Heavy Burdens of Life, the Following Pages—inculcating the Dictates of Simple, Untrammelled Human Nature, are respectfully inscribed by

THE AUTHOR.

INVOCATION.

HAIL Terpsichore, Sweet Goddess of the Dance: Art-Divine! Grace of Manners and Innocent Joys are thy Charming Gifts, Gentle Muse, and not in the Rhythism of Motion, but only in a Bad Heart, or a Vicious Tongue, is the *Guilt of Sin*. Then hail, Terpsichore, Sweet Goddess of the Dance, all hail! Bigots may scowl, Hypochondriacs—Horror-Stricken, may sigh, Dancing is, nevertheless, an Amusement as Old and as Universal as the Human Race. Classic Antiquity made it one of its Chief Modes of Æsthetic Development as well as Most Delightful Pastime, while the Holy Bible of the Jews and the Christians' Sacred Gospel Emphatically and Benignly sanction and sanctify its Judicious Observance! Then hail, Sweet Terpsichore, Goddess of the Dance, hail, all hail!

PREFACE.

Among the indulgences which aspire to the
dignity of a higher grade of diversions, and
which, therefore, justly engage the attention of
mankind, *dancing* may be presumed to rank
among the most ancient, the most genial, and
the most universal.

Like many other joyous manifestations of
human nature, it has its bitter foes no less than
its staunch friends. This discrepancy of judgment depends in a great measure, upon the
stand-point from which this eminently pleasur-
able pastime is contemplated as well as upon
the intelligence and moral culture by which the
persons, who express an opinion upon the subject, are distinguished. Ignorance and knowledge—as is well known, move in diverse and
opposing planes of humanity, and must necessarily view in a different light, the manifold
themes of thought, especially those that apper-

tain to the sentiments and tastes of man, either in his individual or social capacity.

The aim of the present investigation is, to ascertain in what light the species of gymnastic exercise, called *dancing*, is to be considered, and, having pointed out its legitimate and, hence, commendable attributes, cordially indorse the practice of dancing, and heartily recommend it to the observance of all who know how to mingle both *wisely and decorously* the gay with the sad, or sunshine with gloom; and who seasonably no less than prudently lay to heart the hoary but sensible lesson, contained in the third chapter of the Book of Ecclesiastes, in which the philosophic author teaches that as there is " a time to mourn," so there is " *a time to dance!*" And then—as Milton writes,

> " Come and trip it as they go,
> On the light fantastic toe."

WILKES-BARRE, April, 1878.

TABLE OF CONTENTS.

THE PARSON ON DANCING.

THE GENERAL BEARING AND SIGNIFICANCE OF DANCING.

CHAPTER I.

The Definition of Dancing.

DANCING—according to our learned lexicographer, the justly renowned Doctor Webster, is "the act of moving in measured step." This definition, it will be readily perceived, applies chiefly to *artistic* or *educated* dancing, beside which it behooves us to bear in mind, that there are corporeal manifestations of the saltatory art, clearly recognized in the agile acts of *leaping* and *frisking*, which must doubtless be deemed to be the natural and spontaneous expressions of joyous emotions, significant of a buoyant spirit, which is ignorant or careless of the trammels of art or the sanctions of prescriptive rules: they

11

are, I may add, decidedly the instinctive "rough and ready" displays of the soul-stirring, soul-elevating saltatory exercise.

It may also be observed here that, notwithstanding the precedent of very high authority to the contrary, on the definition of the participle *dancing,* this decidedly *human* amusement, emanating from a soul animate with joyful impulses, welling and surging over into outward melodies of life expressions—*Terpsichore rendered visible,* does not always reveal its existence by *leaps and frisks,* or *gambols,* but emphatically by " a *shuffling* of the feet" in unison with the rhythms and accents of the resounding musical strains, uttered either by the voluble human voice, sounded on the tuneful instrument, or even *only felt* in the metrical play of the emotions, elicited by an exuberance of an at once exalted and a beatific sentiment.

Dancing then—as appears from the preceding concise disquisition, is, first, a spontaneous or involuntary, measured *pedal* expression of the joyous outbursts of the soul; and, secondly, a studied and artistic response to the tact and pitch of the voice or the instrument. Whence it follows that instinct and tuition circumscribe the sphere, while they illustrate and define the nature, of the lively and often æsthetic saltatory accomplishment.

Externally, the display of the act, denominated dancing, is often induced by cheerful, harmonic sounds; by the playful demonstrations of happy creatures around us; by the tidings of joyful events; by the transporting influence of enchanting scenery; in brief too, finally, by pleasant, exhilarating conversation, and hope-inspiring fortunes. In addition I remark, that a *set*—in the technical language of Terpsichorean performances, or an *individual*, may dance, and the exercise is genuine, normal dancing, provided it is prompted by joyous or devout emotions—the impulsive and often irresistible overflowings of a hopeful as well as a grateful and happy soul!

The view, which Smith takes, or, at least, seems to indorse, in his interesting and instructive work on "Festivals, Games, and Amusements," in respect to one of the causes—which may be appropriately designated the physical cause, to which the saltatory phenomenon among mankind is due, consists in the hypothesis that there is an existing harmony or a mutual adaptation between the emotional susceptibilities of the soul and an all-pervading subtile fluid in nature, which—by its vibratory waves or pulsations, exciting our sensibilities, produces the lively and emphatically demonstrative action of the dance. The laudable attempt to solve the attractive problem of the practice of dancing—at once so common and so significant among the ameliorating as well as agreeable pastimes of mankind, on principles no less novel than they are erudite, deserves respectful notice in these mirthful pages, and will be here, accordingly, introduced to the close scrutiny of the thoughtful reader : " Under certain vehement emotions," he writes, "more especially those of a pleasant description, all men are, and ever have been, natural, spontaneous, involuntary dancers. The child is but " the father to the man," when in his first leap for joy, he executes *le premier pas la danse,* yielding to the impulses of our common nature without dreaming that the saltatory merriment in which he indulges, and which might not improperly be termed the laughter of the legs, has been solemnly defined to be " the art of expressing the sentiments of the mind or the passions by measures, steps or bounds, that are made in cadence ; by regulated motions of the body, and by graceful gestures ; all performed to the sound of musical instruments, or of the voice."

" The connection that exists between certain sounds and those emotions of the human body, called dancing, is essentially a curious speculation that deserves more inquiry than has hitherto been bestowed upon it. Even between inanimate objects and certain notes, there is a sympathy, if that term may be allowed, which is equally surprising and inexplicable. It is well known that the most massive walls, nay, the solid ground itself, will responsively shake and tremble at particular notes in music. This strongly indicates the presence of some universally-diffused and exceedingly elastic fluid, which is thrown into vibrations by the concussions of the atmosphere upon it, produced by the motions of the sounding body. If these concussions are so strong as to make the large quantity of elastic fluid that is dispersed through a stone wall, or a considerable portion of earth, vibrate, it is no wonder they should have the same effect upon that invisible and exceedingly subtile matter which pervades and seems to reside in our nerves."

" There are some"—continues the author in his new and interesting theory on dancing, " whose nerves are so constructed that they cannot be affected by the sounds which affect others; while there are individuals whose nerves are so irritable that they cannot, without the greatest difficulty sit or stand still when they hear a favorite piece of music played.* It has been conjectured by profound inquiries into such subjects, that all the sensations and passions to which we are subject, depend immediately upon the vibrations excited in the nervous fluid above-mentioned. If this is true, we shall immediately understand the origin

---

* According to Gallini, the inhabitants of the Gold Coast are so passionately fond of dancing, that in the midst of their hardest labor, if they hear a person sing or any musical instrument played, they cannot refrain from dancing. Negroes have been known to cast themselves at the feet of Europeans playing on a fiddle, and entreat them to desist, unless they had a mind to tire them to death, as they could not cease to dance as long as they continued to play.

of the various dances among different nations. One kind of vibration, for instance, excites the passions of anger, pride, &c., which are paramount among warlike nations. The sounds capable of such effects, would naturally constitute their martial music, and dances conformable to it would be simultaneously instituted. Among barbarous people, in particular, this appears to have been an invariable occurrence. Other vibrations of the nervous fluid produce the passions of love, joy, &c., and sounds capable of exciting these particular vibrations, will immediately be formed into music for dances of another kind."

CHAPTER II.

In which is illustrated the Early Characteristic and Prevalence of the Dance: Its Primitive Use being chiefly Liturgic, the Religious Element must be, of Course, eminently Apparent.

THE prolific author just quoted, thus further continues his saltatory researches: " Singing and dancing have prevailed from the creation to the present time, says a very grave inquirer; and they will continue, according to all appearance, till the destruction of our species. How profane soever some may affect to consider this amusement as it is at present conducted, it was at first, and indeed during some thousand years, *a religious ceremony*, as we have already intimated in noticing the festivals of the Jews. Some commentators are of opinion, that every psalm had a distinct dance, appropriated to it. " *In utroque Psalmo, nomine chori, intelligi posse cum certo instrumento homines ad sonum ipsius tripudiantes.*"* In the temples of Jerusalem, Samaria, and Alexandria, a stage for these exercises was erected in one part, thence called the choir, the name of which has been preserved in our churches, and the custom too till within a few centuries. The Cardinal Ximenes revived in his time the practice of Mosarabic masses in the cathedral at Toledo, when the people danced both in the choir and in the nave with great decorum and devotion. Le Père Menestrier, a Jesuit, relates the same thing of some churches in France, in 1682; and Gallini tells us, that at Limoges, not long ago, the people used to dance the round in the choir of the church, which is under the invocation of their patron-saint; and at the end of each psalm, instead of the *Gloria Patri*, they sang

---

* The Hebrew designation of the English phrase, "Songs of Degrees," is *Shir Lammayaloth*. It implies musicians who perform in *chorus*, or who—according to the etymology of the word, *go round*, that is, move in a circle. See the psalms—alluded to in the text, from number one hundred and twenty to one hundred and thirty-four inclusively.—G.

as follows : " St. Marcel ! pray for us, and we
will dance in honor of you."

" From these instances of the liturgic exhibitions of the dance," we may see, continues Smith,
"that the modern sect of fanatics, called Jumpers,
who seem to entertain the strange notion that he
who leaps the highest, is the nearest to heaven,
have abused rather than invented the custom of
religious dancing.*   Nevertheless we cannot see
why any motion of the body should be deemed
incompatible with the feelings and offices of devotion.   Considered as a mere expression of joy,
dancing is no more a profanation than singing,
or than simple speaking; nor can it be thought
in the least more absurd that a Christian should
dance for joy that Jesus Christ has risen from the
dead, than that David danced before the ark,
when it was returned to him after a long absence.†
In these and similar cases, the intention and the
feeling, where they emanate from genuine piety,
must be held to hallow the act.

" The Egyptians too had their solemn dances as
well as the Jews; the principal was their astro-

---

* The Jumpers being clearly *abnormal* in their extravagant
devotion to the sprightly Terpsichore, are noticed here only
by the writer, on account of their connection with the narrative of the text : improprieties in the execution of the dance
whether they are well or ill meant, are alike repudiated in
these pages.—G.

† This saltatory performance of the " Sweet Psalmist," will
be again adverted to in the sequel.—G.

nomical dance; of which the sacrilegious dance around the golden calf was an imitation. From the Jews and Egyptians the practice passed into Greece, where the astronomic dance was adapted to the theater, with chorus, strophe, antistrophe, epode, &c., as we have already remarked in referring to the origin of the drama. In the hands, or, as we should rather say, in the feet of this ingenious and highly civilized people, dancing, which among the barbarians was a mere ungovernable transport, became a regular art, by means of which, through the secret sympathies that cement sound and motion with feeling, any passion whatever could be excited in the minds of the beholders. In this way, effects were produced upon the sensitive Greeks that to our colder temperaments appear almost incredible. At Athens, it is said, that the dance of the Eumenides, or Furies, upon the theater, had so expressive a character as to strike the spectators with irresistible terror; men grown old in the profession of arms trembled; the multitude rushed out; women were thrown into fits; and many imagined they saw in earnest those terrible deities commissioned with the vengeance of heaven, to pursue and punish crimes upon earth. Plato and Lucian both speak of dancing as a divine invention, although in the instance just recorded, it seems to have been perverted to purposes of a rather demoniacal nature."

CHAPTER III.

The Dance viewed in Relation to Clubs, Balls, Women, &c.,
or Terpsichore worshipped among the *Élite* of Society.

THE following agreeable and instructive intelligence is taken from a communication of the
London correspondent of the "New-York Times,"
and published in the "*Philadelphia Weekly* Times"
of December the 22d, 1877: "None of our English
clubs, with rare exceptions"—he writes, " ever
open their doors to the ladies. Receptions, such
as those given by the *Lotos* in New-York, are
unknown here. Country hunt-clubs and Polo-
clubs hardly ever miss a season without giving
a grand ball. On Thursday night the Brighton
Polo-Club signalized themselves in this direction.
They gave a magnificent ball at the Pavilion.*
The stewards were the Duke of Hamilton, the

---

* The Pavilion or Marine Palace is "a fantastic Oriental
or Chinese structure, with domes, minarets, pinnacles, and
Moorish stables, begun for the Prince of Wales in 1784, and
finished in 1827. It is now the property of the corporation of
Brighton, and with its fine pleasure-grounds of above seven
acres, it is devoted to the *recreation* of the inhabitants. * * *
It is a pleasant place of resort, and the daily scene of a large
and fashionable concourse of people, &c."—Chambers's Encyclopædia.—G.

Earl of Aylesford, and Earl De Grey. The German, Russian, Austro-Hungarian, Turkish, Italian, and Belgian Ambassadors are at Brighton just now. They all gave their patronage to the ball. Some of them were present. Brighton has seen nothing so gay this season. Some of the leaders of society and fashion are trying to introduce ladies to club-life. The Twickenham idea is being carried out by the Orleans-Club, in King-street. Unfortunately, Scandal has wagged her tongue considerably about the *Orleans-doings on the Thames,* and ladies of position are as chary about joining the club as their husbands are in introducing them.

There is on foot, I am told, a less ambitious scheme for a ladies' club than that of King-street. The promoters intend to supply a real want in London : an establishment to which a gentleman can take his wife, or his daughters, or other members of his family to supper after the theater, or to dinner before the opera ; a sort of private hotel under good management, where the guests are limited, the viands good, and the wines beyond reproach.

I have seen a list of distinguished and honorable names associated with the scheme, which has the support and approval of many ladies of social position and distinction. Premises are already under survey for the club, which originates with a shrewd and enterprising manager of proprie-

tary clubs, Mr. Russell, the creator of the Temple
and the Hanover-square clubs. If he can help
London to a well-conducted club for ladies and
gentlemen, he will materially add to the attractions of the metropolis."

To judge from the aim and nature of this inspiriting communication, it is evident that the
merry saltatory art has many zealous as well as
distinguished patrons abroad, and that intelligent
people in other lands—though professedly Christians, or, at least, fair types and prominent rep-.
resentatives of Christian nations, believe that
dancing in a proper manner, and on suitable occasions, is not incompatible with the practice of
sound religious principles; and that rational
amusement and true piety are clearly the essential twin-factors of a useful, a contented, and a
happy life!

It would, no doubt, be rash to say that—
though the "Orleans' *doings* on the Thames,"
mentioned above, may have been faulty and even
greatly objectionable, that the dance is evidence
of an inherent proneness to sin in man, nay, that
it is sin *per se!* Where is the good that—under
certain circumstances, may not be perverted to
evil; that is not liable to abuse? Or, as Lord
Sterline writes:

"What thing so good which not some harm may bring!
Even to be happy, is a dangerous thing."

CHAPTER IV.

The Universal Fondness of Rude and Savage Tribes of Mankind for Dancing, does not imply the Fact that Dancing in
Civilized Society, is a Barbarous and Sinful Pastime.

THE extraordinary fondness for the dance,
which universally prevails among peoples in bar-
baric stages of social development, has been
hastily adduced in proof that the sprightly saltatory exercise expressive of the dance, is a rude,
vulgar amusement, quite beneath the notice of
genteel society, and that, hence, persons of education and refinement cannot participate in its
indulgence without imminent peril of moral deg-
radation, or, at least, without putting themselves
upon a level with a low and repellent grade of humanity. But this idea is premature and entirely
erroneous, while it leaves the *Divine* warrant—
plainly and forcibly proclaimed in the circumstance, that it is an undoubted and ineradicable
attribute of human nature, for the legitimate use
and innocent enjoyment of the dance, unimpaired
and in the full strength of its pristine import.

If the wild Indian or the savage Bushman, the
stupid Malayan or the fierce New-Zealander, indulges uncouthly or extravagantly in the emo-

tional expressions of the joyous, often *ecstatic* delights of his yet eminently sensuous soul, he does not in the least disparage the habit of dancing, considered as an innate propensity of the heart, but only shows that his awkward and, perhaps, boisterous method of going through its undefined mazes, or frantic evolutions, is necessarily devoid of the cadences and inflections of the rules of art as well as of the ornate graces, imparted only by the careful discipline and finished punctilios of elegant manners : the young idea having not yet been taught *how to shoot!*

Does the child eat, talk or act like the adult, who is familiar with the etiquette of good breeding? and yet its simple, often rude, infantine traits of character, manifested in the peculiarities of its life, its passions, and its preferences, are strictly normal and appropriate as being the true, incipient announcements of the presence of a higher and more finished humanity in embryo.

We do many things that children do, and differ from them only in this respect, that we do it a little better, a little nicer, and in a little more studied and precise manner than they do. The fact that we dance, does not make us barbarians simply because barbarians too dance, and dancing is a chief feature in their barbarous amusements, for we differ materially from them in this, that our rhythms and impassioned intonations in the practice of the saltatory art, are more exact and expressive than is the case with the manner in which they perform the dance; our joys more regulated and sober; our manners more engaging and appropriate; the postures and gesticulations of our bodies less violent, at the same time that they are more decent, and, therefore, more attractive than the untaught *orchestik* of barbarians.

If I assert that an invincible predisposition for the enjoyment of the delights of the sweet Terpsichorean art, is inborn in human nature, I simply assert a truism, inasmuch as dancing is primarily a strictly involuntary or automatic phenomenon, and, therefore, without it humanity— as it is at present constituted, would be incomplete, a limping, halting microcosm, lacking the finished roundness and symmetry, which now distinguishes it as a happy intermixture of the luscious with the bitter, the jovial and the smiling with the doleful and the grim : nature affects harmonious sounds, and virtuous pleasure "drives dull care away." When votaries of the dance, "leap and frisk about," and, tripping gayly, "move nimbly up and down :" it is your mission as much as it is your mission to eat, drink, sleep, walk or run; to sit, labor, rest, laugh or weep. God has wisely ordained that all the faculties with which he has endowed us, should be exercised in their proper time, and in their appropriate manner!

The following Shakespearean view of the gleeful mood, surging and frothing into expressions of the buoyant dance, must be indorsed by all sensible and liberal-minded people, who love— now and then, to behold a bright and cloudless sky, or to bask in the genial rays of sunny life:

> " The man that hath not music in himself,
>   Nor is not moved with concord of sweet sounds,
>   Is fit for treason, stratagems, and spoils."

———

CHAPTER V.

The Important Sanitary Effects of Dancing upon the Mental and Physical Constitution of Man.

THE indulgence in the nimble, shuffling mazes of the sprightly dance may, indeed, be carried to excess, or it may expend itself in careless and blamable disregard of the hurtful influences which sometimes slyly and wickedly beset its devious paths, and, hence, the merry offerings of the saltant chorus to the gay and supple goddess of the leaping rhythms and impassioned cadences, may prove to be an evil instead of a good; a reason why it should be diligently borne in mind, that the abuse of a practice or institution, which is not in itself reprehensible or deleterious, and which—under certain wise and timely restrictions, may exert a most salutary as well as necessary sway over the delicate and wonderfully complex human organism, by no means—as has been already stated, furnishes a valid argument for its condemnation and disuse. The disgusting vice of gluttony cannot afford an adequate reason for the interdiction of a proper, temperate participation of food; and an excessive use of strong drink—the reproach and guilt of the thirsty worshippers of Bacchus! can never be deemed to be a well-founded objection against the moderate, that is, properly speaking, *medicinal or hygienic* indulgence in spirituous liquors. The German adage, " Das mittel Masz ist die beste Strasz," is —in most cases, a safe rule both for our dietetic behavior and physical recreations.

Dancing—when it is neither excessive nor too protracted, is naturally a bracing and healthful exercise. By the alternate contraction and relaxation of the muscles as well as the quickened flow of the nervous fluid, the various parts of the body are pleasantly and congenially impressed. Owing to these facts, the numerous functions of the body are discharged with greater ease and vigor, while a thrill of delight passes through the soul, which—in its reaction upon the physical organs, increases the amount of pleasant sensations, and, hence, enlarges the sphere of general well-being.

From the preceding premises, it may be inferred that dancing: the *measured steps* and due

inflections of the passions in honor of Terpsichore,
the charming saltant goddess, is really one of the
chief life-cordials of the human race. For beside
the commendable qualities—already noticed, in
which it is emphatically conspicuous, it attests its
further usefulness in a sanitary point of view, by
promoting the secretion of the gastric juice; by
facilitating the peristaltic motions of the intes-
tines; by stimulating the action of the absorb-
ents; and by thus materially aiding in animalizing
and assimilating the food adapted for the nutri-
ment of man.

Dancing, moreover, has the merit of opening
the pores of the body—often clogged by effete
matter, and of being, therefore, instrumental in
the copious discharge of insensible perspiration :
thus, no doubt, opportunely ridding the system
of the latent germs of disease. To these sanitary
virtues of the dance, I may add that it likewise
expands the breast, accelerates the circulation of
the blood; causes a more rapid removal of the
carbonic acid from the venous tubes; and, consequently, the more abundant inhalation of oxy-
gen gas, so essential to the health and life of the
human family.

Finally, kept under prudent control, dancing
is a useful and exhilarating pastime amid the
many vexing and depressing cares, incident to
our daily existence, and hence, as such, it is a
seasonable and welcome dispeller of mental

gloom; an effectual balm to the wounded and
frequently bleeding heart; the facile mover of
innocent mirth and genuine laughter: it loves
harmless wit and pleasant jokes, in place of stale
monotony and melancholy brooding; in short, it
is a more efficacious *elixir of life* than has ever been
distilled in the *alembic*, or that has ever been found
among the panaceas of quacks!

CHAPTER VI.

The Dance considered as a Potent and Agreeable Means to
soften the Manners, and refine the Pleasures and Tastes of
Social Intercourse.

ACCORDING to Webster, "Music is a combina-
tion of simultaneous sounds in accordance or
harmony." Such being the case, it evidently in-
cludes both the saltatory art and æsthetics, or the
science of taste and the beautiful, inasmuch as
the artistic or educated display of the rhythms
and mazes of the dance, is eminently a performance full of symmetry and grace, abounding—in
its more appropriate sphere and manner of expression, in the bland amenities and the chief
charms of polished society: contemplated in
these various relations, the dance is clearly an
important branch of the liberal arts as well as an
effective means of education.

The proposition, which it is proposed to vindicate in this chapter, is, that the party-dance—not the extempore and anomalous amusement recognized under that name, cultivated and perfected among the upper ranks of society, has a decidedly elevating and ameliorating influence upon the character and the well-being of the more thoughtful and discreet votaries of the fair and gleeful muse of the saltatory art.

To appear at a select, or, at least, a respectable social gathering, the commendable object of which is friendly and urbane intercourse, and mutual, virtuous enjoyment, seems necessarily to premise a wise and careful preparation; a diligent attention to what is seemly and proper on the jocund and distinguished occasion, or—in other words, to what will likely be deemed by the party either as genteel or vulgar, and, consequently, as furthering or hindering the object of the purposed enjoyment and coveted recreation.   Hence the dancer's motto should be, They that would derive pleasure from others' intercourse, must feel under obligation to reciprocate the enjoyment.   A neglect of this duty, at once so natural and so reasonable, is sure to end in deserved grief and disappointment.

To an appropriate and decent mingling in the social dance, *formally* inaugurated by respectable parties, who—it is to be taken for granted, are sufficiently removed from the scum and dregs of society to occupy a higher plane in civilization, the idea of giving timely and assiduous thought to personal cleanliness, must—it seems, arise spontaneously in the educated mind, and be, at once, urgent and unavoidable; for it is very evident that without it, a lively conviction must be felt that the claim to gentility will be denied, and the right to equal companionship absolutely refused, it being plainly a glaring dereliction of good manners, both offensive to correct taste as well as impolitic on the score of self-interest. An instinctive sense of propriety likewise dictates the strict observance of the conventional canons of polite behavior; of friendly attentions to the wants of others; and of studious care to guard against too great sensitiveness under provocation or insult, lest the title to a proper self-respect should be irretrievably forfeited.

It is evident too, I may remark, that the joyous children of the nimble-footed divinity, will consider it a duty of primary importance to appear amid the glad, expectant throng, where beauty and gallantry, grace and dignity, are presumed to greet and delight each other, habited in appropriate and well-made clothes, with the addition of such ornate appendages as are especially suitable for ladies, who naturally and properly love the elegant as well as the useful in dress.

Good taste; seasonable counsel; and a fixed purpose to be agreeable and to please, will sel-

dom fail accurately to guide the discriminating
votary of the dance, in the choice of what is
seemly in color; suitable in quality; neat and
strictly adapted, according to the received canons
of dress, observed in the ornate costume of the
gay and graceful toilet of the saltant and thrice-
charming goddess:

> " There is nothing in the world like etiquette
> In kingly chambers, or imperial halls,
> As also at the race, and country balls."—BYRON.

Knowledge too constitutes an important part
in the necessary preparation of the pleasure-seeking dancers on the all-absorbing ball-occasion,
when the " light, fantastic toe" shall, perhaps,
sport most nimbly, or frisk the gayest and the
prettiest. To be deficient in commonplace intelligence under circumstances plainly challenging
mutual emulation, in the presence of a chosen
assemblage of ladies and gentlemen, all, most
probably, intent on excelling in different kinds
of useful or elegant knowledge, as well as studious in the use of expressions, which imply
familiarity of polite breeding, would ill become
the ambitious votaries of the inspiriting and
genial amusement, designated the dance.

The dancer, in most cases, is, indeed, keenly
aware of the facts, referred to in the last paragraph, and, hence, while he diligently refreshes
his memory from past studies, he assiduously

strives to enrich his mind with such discoveries of recent researches as the anticipated opportunity may likely render necessary, as a test of mental culture and social position. In short, each of the joyous band, innately conscious of the apparently divinely-ordained mission of the dance, to exercise an emphatically softening and refining influence upon the lovers of innocent pleasure, as well as the friends of sound health and a cheerful mind, they will wisely. aim to shine; to please; and to be, at once, an honor and an ornament in the midst of the happy *coterie*, where the polite dancer should expect to find that rich treasure, "The feast of reason, and the flow of soul." Or—such is the elevating tendency of the elegant and delightful saltatory pastime, that they will naturally strive after the Byronic goal :

"Longings sublime and aspirations high."

Terpsichore is often fervently invoked by parents of education and taste, to impart her lovely and graceful attributes — as finishing "touches," to the accomplishments of their children, and the remark is often made with marked emphasis, that it is readily apparent from the easy, buoyant gait, and the erect, symmetrical bearing of some favored individuals, that they have taken lessons in the courtly school of the agreeable, nimble-footed, most urbane, and most charming divinity of the divine dance!

Locke—the celebrated philosopher, in his "Treatise on Education," thus pertinently and sensibly speaks of the refining influence of the dance : "Dancing," says the philosopher, "being that which gives graceful motions to all our limbs, and, above all things, manliness and a becoming confidence to young children, I think, cannot be learned too early. Nothing appears to me to give children so much self-possession and behavior, and so to raise them to the conversation of those above their years, as dancing."

Ruskin—styled in the annals of English literature, "the most eloquent and original of all writers upon art," has, according to the Philadelphia Weekly Times, come to the conclusion : which may be a little startling to the morose votaries of asceticism, that "music and *precise dancing* are, after all, the only safeguards of morality."

SECTION II.

THE DANCE AMONG THE ANCIENT HEATHENS.

CHAPTER I.

Examples of Their Military Dances.

PARAGRAPH I.

The Spartans and the Pyrrhic Dance.*

OF the importance attached to the amusement of the dance by the ancients, we may judge from the fact that it engaged the serious attention of Plato, who reduces the dances of the Greeks, for example, to three classes. 1. The military dances, which tended to make the body robust, active, and well disposed for all the exercises of war; 2. The domestic dances, which had for their object an agreeable and innocent recreation and amusement; and, 3. The mediatorial dances, which were used in expiations and sacrifices.

The Spartans had introduced a military dance

---

* Under this head, the *Games*, *Festivals*, and *Amusements*, once more solicit the respectful attention of the reader.

for the purpose of early exciting the courage of
their children, and of leading them on insensibly
to the exercise of the armed dance.   This children's dance, which used to be executed in the
public place, was composed of two choirs, the
one of grown men, the other of children; whence,
being chiefly designed for the latter, it took its
name.   The choir of the children regulated their
motions by those of the men, and all danced at
the same time, singing the poems of Thales, Alc-
man, and Dionysadotus.

The Pyrrhic dance was performed by young
men, *completely armed*, who executed to the sound
of the flute all the proper movements either for
attack or defence.   It was composed of four parts:
the first, the *podism*, or footing, which consisted
in a quick shifting motion of the feet, such as
was necessary for overtaking a fleeing enemy, or
for getting away from him when he proved to be
an overmatch.   The second part was the *xiphism:*
this was a kind of mock-fight, in which the
dancers imitated all the motions of combatants;
aiming a stroke, darting a javelin, or dexterously
dodging, parrying, or avoiding a blow or thrust.
The third part, called the *homos*, consisted in very
high leaps, or vaultings, which the dancers frequently repeated, for the better using themselves
occasionally to leap a ditch, or spring over a wall.
The *tetracomos*, the fourth and last part, was a
square figure, executed by slow and majestic

movement; but it is uncertain whether this was everywhere performed in the same manner or not.

Of all the Greeks, the Spartans were those who most cultivated the Pyrrhic dance. This warlike people exercised their children in it, from the age of five years, to the accompaniment of hymns and songs. The following piece was sung at the dance, called *Trichoria*, from the fact that it was composed of three choirs—one of children, another of young men, and the third of the aged. The latter *opened* the dance, saying, "In time past we were valiant." The young men answered, "We are so *at present*." To which the chorus of children replied, "We shall be still more so when *our* time comes."

The Spartans never danced but with real arms. In process of time, however, other nations came to use weapons of wood on such occasions. Nay, it was only so late as the time of Athenæus, who lived in the second century, that the dancers of the Pyrrhic saltatorial exercise, instead of arms, carried only flasks, ivy-bound wands, or reeds. But even in Aristotle's time, they had begun to use thyrsuses instead of pikes, and lighted torches instead of javelins and swords, with which they executed a dance, denominated the conflagration of the world.*

---

* It may be observed here—as an interesting fact, that among the ancients, there were neither festivals nor religious

PARAGRAPH II.

Bellona, the Goddess of War, and Patron of Martial Sports.

The daring goddess Bellona has largely figured in the mythic annals of antiquity as the
goddess of war, and the companion, or—as is

---

ceremonies, which were not accompanied with songs and
dances.   It was not held possible to celebrate any mystery, or
to be initiated in any sacred institution, without the intervention of the two arts—the song and the dance.—G.

"The Pyrrhic Dance," as appears from Chambers's Encyclopædia, "the most famous of all the war-dances of antiquity,
is said to have received its name from one Pyrrichos, or, according to others, from Pyrrhus or Neoptolemus, the son of
Achilles.   Critical scholars, however, content themselves with
a general inference deduced from the substantial harmony of
the various mythical or legendary accounts given of its origin
—viz., that it was a *Doric* invention.   It was danced to the
flute, and its time was both quick and light, as may be seen
from the Pyrrhic foot, composed of two shorts—∪∪, and the
Prokeleusmatic,* or challenging-foot, of two double shorts—
∪∪ ∪∪.   According to Plato, it aimed to represent the nimble
motion of a warrior either avoiding missiles and blows, or as-
saulting the enemy ; and in the Doric States, it was as much a
piece of military training as an amusement.   Elsewhere, in
Greece, it was purely a mimetic dance, in which the parts
were sometimes represented by women.   It formed part of
the public entertainments at the Panathénaic festivals.   Ju-
lius Cæsar introduced it at Rome, where it became a great
favorite," &c.

---

* Derived from the Greek *Prokéleusmatikòs*, signifying a metrical
foot of four short syllables.—G.

affirmed by some, the sister, and by others, the wife, of Mars, the puissant god and valiant professor of the same belligerent and bloody art, as that to which herself was emphatically devoted. Her euphonic name is, doubtless, derived from the Latin substantive, *Bellum*, denoting war, while its deduction from the Greek term, *Bellona*, meaning a needle, of which she is said, according to Tooke, to have been the inventress, boasts its advocates and claims our notice.

Already at an early period of the cultivation of the fine arts, the æsthetic and imaginative Greeks represented the martial goddess in the rival productions of the painter and the sculptor, and she, hence, assumed a prominent rank among the leading divinities that elicited the pious regard and received the devout homage of the heathen world.

The fair and warlike goddess appeared clad in complete armor; bearing a burning torch in her hand; her hair flowing in unrestrained luxuriance and wild profusion over her ample shoulders, while she rushed through the battle array of her followers, and in tones of fervent eloquence, animated the sturdy warriors to deeds of bravery, or seasonably inspired them with the ardent and impetuous hope of triumph.

Her priests were the famous *Bellonarii*. Armed —as became their martial pursuit, with swords and—simulating the ardor and fierceness of battle, they pierced their bodies with wounds, and presented the blood, which was thus shed, as a grateful offering to the stern and decidedly pugnacious goddess. In the discharge of their *saltatory* functions, they moved up and down in two ranks, observing the prescribed measures and evolutions according to the received canons of the military dance, sacred to their tutelar divinity.

This military dance—it may be remarked, was a *choral or ring-dance*, which traces its derivation to the Greek word *Xoròs*, and was composed of the strophe and the antistrophe-movement, with a slight halt before the altar, called the *epode*. Its purpose evidently was to emblematize the earth's path through the tropics, and its presumed momentary suspension of rotation at the equator : the dividing *line* between the northern and the southern hemispheres of the globe. It was strictly an astronomical dance, and like all the dances of a similar character, it is to be regarded as the origin and type of the present widely prevailing and exquisitely enjoyed *Waltz : ünder allen Tänzen*, des Deŭtchen *höchstes Vergnügen!*

PARAGRAPH III.

Mars, the Valiant God of War, and the Martial, Liturgic Rites, dedicated to his Services.

Mars—in Greek *"Ares*, is the puissant god of war, the untiring champion of justice, and the benign and potent fructifier of the earth. He bears also the distinguished cognomen *Gradivus* —from *a gradiendo in bella*, because with rapid pace, he hastens to battle.

The annual festival of Mars, was celebrated with numerous ceremonies and solemn pomp, on the first day of the sacred month of March, which still bears his name and perpetuates his memory. On that day began the new-year among the ancient people of Italy. At a later age, this venerable anniversary celebration was transferred by Numa—it is said, to the first of January: a name derived from the god *Janus*, and thenceforth inscribed on the first month of the year in the future calendar.

The priests of Mars—it is to be observed, were the widely renowned *Salii*, whose sacerdotal origin is clearly traceable to an Oriental source. One of the distinguished duties of the Salii—as will further appear in the sequel, was to chant the devout praises to the divine beings, strictly and appropriately designated as the *martial gods*.

Dionysius Halicarnassus, according to Creut-

zer,* deduces the name Salii directly from the
Greek *Koúretes*, the same as *Curetes*, in Latin, and
meaning an *altar*, in the original called *Koŭros*.
Whence we can readily recognize the derivation
of the terms *chorus*, *choral*, and *choir*, all implying
a circle or roundness—the shape of the altar.
On the contrary, the Latins explain the name of
the Salic priests from their saltant military exercises—or *salire*, to dance.   In either case, however, the primary import and intention of their
institution, was to symbolize in the choral or
round, military dances, the spherical motion of
the planets, and the periodic revolutions of time.

The first in rank—among the Salii, was the
præsul, or dancing-master, whose weighty office
it was to conduct the choral, military dance, and
to make all the necessary arrangements for the
saltant exercises. Next to him succeed in priority
of importance, the *vates*, whose business it especially was to superintend the proper rendering
of the sacred hymns.   Over the whole body of
the Salic priest-hood—the Salii, just mentioned,
included, presided the *magister collegi Saliorum*.

No one could become a member of the illustrious order of Salic priests, unless he was of pa-
tristic descent: a condition which seems to have

---

* The writer of these pages gratefully acknowledges his
obligation for the aid he has received in some parts of his
labors from Creutzer's elaborate work, "Die Symbolik und
Mythologie der Alten Völker, besonders der Griechen."

been scrupulously observed among the Romans to the last days of the Republic. Besides, at the time of his initiation into the order, it was deemed essential that both his parents should be still alive.

The splendid robes, which officially distinguished the Salii, consisted mainly of embroidered and versi-colored tunics—tunica *picta,* while a cap, called *apex,* much resembling the outlines of a helm, and coming to a sharp point in the crown, covered their venerable and sacred heads. This head-gear was on some occasions dispensed with, and a cowl—according to the Gabinian custom, substituted, when : thus habited, they were wont to carry the celebrated *ancilia,* or sacred shields of Mars, in martial procession and solemn pomp.

On the first of March, the happy birth-day of the new-year, the Salii, clad in their ornate, martial robes, in merry and boldly expressed rhythms, performed the impressive military dance : the grand liturgic rite of the fiery Mars, and sang— agreeably to Ovid, in his Poem on the Roman festivals, the warlike odes, pertinent to the important occasion.

The martial exercises, performed on the nativity of the new-year, were the significant preludes of the approaching military campaign, and the consequent march of the army in pursuit of the foe : war among the ancients, was notoriously the paramount business of the State. According to a long established custom among belligerent nations, the campaign opened when the fields began to be decked with herbage, and horse and rider could encamp without harm or inconvenience, in the open air.

It was too on the first day of March, sacred to the annual revolution of time, that the Salii, imitating their god, who presided over war and the seasons, began their heroic exercises in the Field of Mars—the famous *Campus Martius*, not failing to accompany them with the usual *war-dance*, and while marching in military array, bearing aloft the heaven-sent ancilia : before noticed, which they alternately shook and struck as they continued to advance, and thus, in ecstatic mood, and the lively chanting of the martial hymns, they vigorously moved in the expressive choral dance: emphatically an astronomical dance, and, therefore, of deep symbolical import.

The hymns which the Salii sang in energetic strains, during the celebration of the important day, sounded the praises of the immortal gods, while they expressed the honorable reminiscence of the favored mortals, who—by heroic deeds and noble daring, had justly earned a title to a place after death, among the martial divinities, and would be, besides, the pleasing themes of hearty Salic song and sonorous Salic dance, while —according to Byron, there shall endure,

" Battle's magnificently stern array."

CHAPTER II.

Examples of Purely Religious Dances among the Ancient
Heathens.

PARAGRAPH I.

Pan, the Divine Dancer, and the Supreme Patron of the Saltatory Art.

THOUGH—owing chiefly to the extravagant and
ridiculous tales of idle poets and other silly de-
famers of the mythic gods, the god *Pan* may
appear with somewhat diminished luster in the
later and gravely corrupt religeo-symbolic literature of antiquity, there can be no reasonable
doubt—after a candid and thorough investigation of the subject, that, viewed in the light of
an orthodox and normal contemplation of him
by his worshippers, Pan justly ranked as the
first and the greatest of the gods, and is, hence,
deservedly as well as emphatically designated
Father Pan!

The designation Pan, denoting *totality*, is fitly
borne by the sacred and exalted being, to whom
this paragraph is properly dedicated, because—
as Tooke supposes in his " Pantheon of the Gods,"
etc., " he exhilarated the minds of all the gods
with the music of his famous reed-pipe : an ingenious specimen of his inventive talent, as well

as by the exquisite harmony of the more finished lyre, on which he is said to have played with marked skill and wonderful effect as soon as he was born ! Or, perhaps, he is called Pan, because he governed the whole world by his mind as he symbolized it by his body."

In his choral or ring-dances, Pan—as the master-waltzer of the merry saltant host, either of men or the immortal gods, strikingly expressed the nature and rapidity of the different planetary motions. In an ode on Pan, by Pindar, the great lyric poet of Greece, this pre-eminently saltant as well as musical deity, is forcibly described as the *Dancer!*

The evident propriety of the bestowal of this title upon Pan, is promptly reiterated and confirmed in the following quotation by Aristides, honorably surnamed the "Just:" "Pindar," he writes, "calls Pan the dancer and the most exalted of the gods." A truth which the Egyptian priests as well as the priests everywhere—versed in profound mythic lore, readily recognize and perpetuate." Creutzer pertinently adds : "We perceive by a reference to the context of the "Third Pythian Ode," that distinct notice is taken of Pan's orchestral proficiency no less than of his illustrious rank among the rest of the gods : dogmas, which have been widely promulgated by Herodotus—the renowned *Father of History*, in his celebrated treatise on the Egyptian gods."

When astronomy began to be cultivated with some success and the zodiac was introduced into the calendar of the husband-man, the year in the northern hemisphere of the globe, opened at the time of the vernal equinox, or in the sign of the *ram*, it being the season when sheep yean, and, accordingly, a statue or some other representation of the ram, as the appropriate symbol of the fleecy ovine herd, was adopted as a suitable means of typifying and perpetuating this interesting and important fact. In the course of time, the people lost sight of the design and import of this clearly astronomical institution, and instead of henceforth considering the ram as a mere significant symbol, regarded it as a *god*, and the *creator* of the seemingly boundless solar system. Pan was, therefore, no longer simply a zodiacal sign or a zodiacal god, but the sole and most potent Sun-God!

Passing over his strictly *Ariel* insignia, in silence, I remark that Pan presented himself before his numerous and zealous worshippers, with a pine-wreath, ornately encircling his venerable head; a shepherd's crook in one hand, and a reed-pipe in the other. With the wonderful music which he performed upon this primitive instrument, it is affirmed, he cheered even the gods themselves. The nymphs—fair and blithe creatures, seduced by the ecstasy of the divine harmony, danced in precise and measured time to the sweet tones of the rude pastoral pipe, just mentioned, composed of seven tubes of unequal length, and significant of the heavenly music of the planetary spheres. Finally, Pan wore a spotted robe, the symbol of the starry firmanent which—it was believed, reflected his creative power!

Creutzer, the learned mythologist, already mentioned, "says this extraordinary musical pipe of Pan, had a profound cosmic import. For it was the exact resonance of the exquisite harmony of which that god alone could be the exhaustless source, and, hence, the seven pipes denoted the seven planets, the shortest implying the pale moon, and the longest, the remote and belted Saturn. In short, Pan was—agreeably to mythic lore, the radiant and resplendent fountain of all planetary light as well as the grand key-note of planetary harmony!

Among almost innumerable places of worship, sacred to Pan, that god had a temple in Rome, at the foot of the Palatine hill; his festivals— among the Roman people, are known as the Lupercalia, while his priests figured under the name of the Luperci: designations which are evidently—as will readily be perceived, more euphonious than attractive. Beside the statue of Pan, burned a perpetual fire, the miniature-symbol of the bright and glorious sun. I will only add, that for many ages, the worship of Pan could boast a world-wide and spontaneous recognition.

The *orchestik* talents of Pan, and especially his extraordinary dancing capacities, commend the science of harmonical sounds and the accurate no less than pleasing art of the figurative dance, to our careful attention, while they abundantly justify our imitation of pastimes, which have descended to us thus evidently sanctified and exalted. What, the great cosmic god of antiquity, Pan, should make the noble art of dancing a main pursuit of his divine life, and, hence, rank as the sweetest as well as the most consummate *dancer*, either among gods or men, and mortals, endowed by the Almighty with propensities for enjoyment, and absolutely needing seasonable relaxation and recreation to ensure a sound and normal condition of both the mental and the physical functions of their divine and wonderful frames, should be debarred from the proper indulgence in a practice, at once so pleasant and so beneficial, because fanatics disapprovingly shake their addled heads, or hypocrites— for the sake of worldly gain, feign a pious horror of the saltatory art? No, for shame, *No!*

The ancient heathens hardly ever worshipped unless they also danced; for the dance was in most cases a salient part of the divine service, fitly consisting of pleasure and solemnity: Pan— the celestial dancer, had everywhere his admiring and zealous disciples, and this cheerful and pleasant kind of sacred cultus does by no means imply

that all the devout dancers in the worship of Pan,
were fools or sensualists, but that they understood
—like sensible people to appreciate the advantage
of enjoying the *sunny-side of life!* May but the
dancer's watch-word be the apostolic injunction:
Let all things be done decently and in order, and
then let him boldly defy alike the surly grum-
bler and the narrow-minded bigot! Goldsmith,
I finally remark, has struck the true vein in the
queenly saltatory amusement, and thus sings the
praises of the dance:

> " Alike all ages; dames of ancient days
> Have led their children through the mirthful maze;
> And the gay grandsire, skill'd in gestic lore,
> Has frisk'd beneath the burden of three-score."

PARAGRAPH II.

Religious Dances among the Ancients, Expressive chiefly of Joy and
Gratitude.

Among the most common and agreeable
amusements of the æsthetic Greeks,* were music
and dancing: twin sisters, justly ranking with
the *liberal arts* as well as being the chief delight
of the gods. As an important element in pleas-
urable pastime, music seldom failed to be employed at religious festivals and social banquets,

---

· * For a part of this and the next paragraph, I own my-
self indebted to Fiske's interesting and instructive " Classical
Antiquities."

which were—as may easily be presumed, the classic and exceedingly appropriate occasions for the introduction of the exhilarating dance, performed as a solo or in concert, yet always according to the rules of art and " *in figure.*"

Beside the saltatory exhibitions at such happy times, it was customary to associate—during the intervening stages of its exercises, various sports and gymnastic displays; as, leaping, running, riding, wrestling, and the like. These eminently athletic episodes of the dance, must necessarily have confined them to the amusement of the more robust and supple sex, who alone could enjoy and might appreciate them. The same remark and illustration will apply to the pastime, in which dancing and playing at *ball—sphaĭra,* were practiced consecutively, and hence, probably, with enhanced zest.

At weddings the timid and bashful bride was conducted to her future home, by the gallant bride-groom, with all the component elements of distinguished pomp and great rejoicing. In this jubilant and felicitous procession, torches— premising, of course, a night-scene, were borne with sprightly air and agile steps, before the newly-married couple, while nuptial hymns were sung by a happy and smiling retinue of youths and virgins, buoyant themselves with hope, and cheered by bright anticipations of the future. Dancing—saltant child of fair and nimble Terpsichore, customarily formed a prominent as well as pleasing part of the hymeneal rites, while savory, festive banquets fitly closed and magnified the delightful event.

Singing — *molpè*, instrumental music, and dancing: *'orchestùs*, being the lively and genteel accompaniments of their festive entertainments, attest the æsthetic and sprightly genius of Hellenic civilization. In most instances, the songs in early times were chiefly hymns to the gods, or those heroes that seemed most in their actions, to reflect the nature and the dignity of the gods. In subsequent ages, songs and dances of a less chaste, and, therefore, questionable character, once in awhile, invaded the legitimate sphere of sober, rational amusements: a fact, which implies abuse of these noble arts as well as deterioration of taste, and justly elicits disapprobation among the friends of innocent and legitimate enjoyments.

After the conclusion of the charming, affiliated recreations—music and the dance, it was a popular custom to invite the guests to finish the delightful exercises, in which they had hitherto indulged, by finally participating in various other pleasant and healthful pastimes, and thus agreeably diversifying and prolonging the rational enjoyments of the gay and happy occasion.

The preceding details are convincing evidence that the Greeks—celebrated among the nations

of antiquity, for their devotion to the elements
of the beautiful and the sensitive in human development, knew well to appreciate and to enjoy
social pleasures and amusements. Accordingly,
we find the sources from which these striking
national peculiarities were derived, to have been
as numerous as they were copious and abiding,
and that, in the more flourishing periods of their
interesting and instructive history, they exercised
an eminently refining and elevating influence,
which far exceeded any other agency in Hellenic
progress in arts and learning.

Among so æsthetic and sprightly a race of
people, it must be, indeed, self-evident that music
and dancing held the most prominent place in
every pursuit and relaxation, appertaining to
practical life, and were absolutely essential to the
proper celebration and just éclat of all festivals,
either public or private, as well as all friendly
gatherings and polite entertainments.

In the fond and diligent observances of these
decidedly most humanizing and ameliorating
customs, we are told, there was a due regard not
merely to immediate gratification—usually the
end and aim of the vicious and the vulgar, but
pre-eminently to the weightier and more glorious
ends of promoting general culture, and a more
lovely and engaging as well as a more perfect,
efficient, and enduringly happy humanity!

Finally, Cupid too deserves an honorable place

in these jocund pages.   He is, it seems, the illustrious son of Jupiter and Venus.   His birth is,
therefore, divine, and his august mission among
men, is the cultivation of the tender and pretty
plant, called *love*.   He is a very sly divinity, and
quite full of harmless or mischievous pranks.
Besides, he is the graceful and facile bearer of
the *golden dart* as well as of the ample quiver,
replenished with sharp and fatal arrows.   The
bland, sportive little being has rendered himself
famous among the gods, by his marvellous skill
in the associate arts of music and the dance.   He
is, hence, emphatically the *winged-dancer*, and the
only lover, whether human or divine—as far as is
known to the writer, who first *shoots* his fair and
confiding victim, and then marries her : showing
that love when it is well-matured, is a violent
passion and often produces a species of madness !
In this most extraordinary love-trait, Cupid strikingly differs from many enamored mortals, who
first *caress* and afterwards *break the heart*, of the
erst loved and fondled one !

Farewell Cupid, beautiful winged-dancer !
May you live always and be ever astir ; ever ma-
ture honest love ; ever nimbly, sweetly sing and
joyously move in the choral dance ; nay, ever
play the *gay*, the *grave* hymeneal rôle.

Our theme not being exhausted, it still admits
of the further, following expansion.—In the eigh-
teenth book of the Iliad, it is thus that Homer,

Greece's immortal poet, commemorates the blessings of the " brown sheaves of corn," and the luscious fruit of the vintage.   Let us learn how —with rural banquet, merry song, and happy dance or gestic glee, an ancient and venerable *harvest-home* was fitly celebrated :

"Another field rose high with waving grain ;
With bended sickles stand the reaper-train :
Here stretch'd in ranks the levell'd swarths are found,
Sheaves heap'd on sheaves here thicken up the ground.
With sweeping stroke the mowers strow the lands ;
The gatherers follow, and collect in bands ;
And last the children, in whose arms are borne
(Too short to gripe them) the brown sheaves of corn.
The rustic monarch of the field descries
With silent glee the heaps around him rise.
A ready banquet on the turf is laid,
Beneath an ample oak's expanded shade.
The victim ox the sturdy youths prepare ;
The reaper's due repast, the women's care.
Next, ripe in yellow gold, a vine-yard shines,
Bent with the ponderous harvest of its vines ;
A deeper dye the dangling clusters show,
And, curl'd on silver props, in order glow :
A darker metal mix'd intrench'd the place ;
And pales of glittering tin the' enclosure grace.
To this, one pathway gently winding leads,
Where march a train with baskets on their heads—
Fair maids and blooming youths, that smiling bear
The purple product of th' autumnal year.
To these a youth awakes the warbling strings,
Whose tender lay the fate of Linus sings ;*

---

* According to Mythology, Linus lost his life by the homicidal deed of Hercules.—G.
The following extract from the " Sketches of Rural Customs

In measured dance behind him move the train,
Tune soft the voice, and answer to the strain.
A figur'd dance succeeds : such once was seen
In lofty Gnosus, for the Cretan queen,
Form'd by Dædalean art : a comely band
Of youths and maidens, bounding hand in hand.
The maids in soft simars of linen dress'd ;
The youths all graceful in the glossy vest :
Of those the locks with flowery wreaths enroll'd :
Of these the sides adorn'd with swords of gold,

---

and People in the Land of Homer," may be appropriately
noticed in this place :

"That ancient custom, dancing—it might almost be called
worship, of the Greeks," writes the author, "is as popular as
ever among the peasants, and no festival-day passes without
its indulgence.   The graceful, supple forms suit it admirably,
and some are always renowned for their skill in leading the
chorus and for the lightness of their steps.   It seems easy
exercise, but is really very complicated.   Thirty or forty
young men collect in the open air, and joining hands form a
line, advancing, bending, unrolling, extending, and pressing
together, obedient to the cadenced rhythm of a song which
they all repeat.   The voices rise and fall as the steps are slow
or quick.   At times the *pilikari* who heads the chain gives a
signal, when each lets go his neighbor's hand, which he held
above his head, turns around, and takes that of the one following, and so on through the circle.   The rich costumes and
variegated colors make a scene of changing beauty : it is the
ancient *ormos*, of which classic authors speak, and though
there exist many other dances, this is the most popular, and
has been transmitted for ages with perfect fidelity.   The
higher classes seldom consent to mix in choruses so dear to
their ancestors : the waltz and the quadrille have taken the
place, and real European balls are frequently given in all the
towns, which have few attractions for those who are in search
of originality."

That, glittering gay, from silver belts depend.
Now all at once they rise, at once descend,
With well-taught feet: now shape, in oblique ways,
Confus'dly regular, the moving maze:
Now forth at once, too swift for sight, they spring,
And undistinguish'd blend the flying ring:
So whirls a wheel, in giddy circle tost,
And, rapid as it runs, the single spokes are lost.
The gazing multitudes admire around:
Two active tumblers in the center bound;
Now high, now low, their pliant limbs they bend :
And general songs the sprightly revel end.''

PARAGRAPH III.

Showing that the Dances of the Ancient Heathens had a decidedly
Religious Character, it made no Matter what the Cultus or the
Occasion might be : a Summary of Facts will illustrate and confirm
the Proposition.

The nations of antiquity, who had outgrown
the barbarous state of the civil polity, seem to
have understood much better how to avail themselves of the true conditions of a joyous and
happy existence, than is the case with a large
portion of the present inhabitants of the globe.

We find among them, therefore, no ignoble
moping or melancholy brooding over misfortunes
or wrongs. On the contrary, they present themselves generally before us as contented, glad,
and happy beings, who, if adversity or sorrow
happened to mar and ruffle the bright and placid
outlines of their lives, readily found means to
escape from harm or alleviate their troubles : the

sovereign hygienic remedy being—in every case, a resort to the magic power of music and the dance! Indeed, all their devotional exercises, all their domestic and social transactions, partook in an eminent degree of a musical and saltatory character, and the feet were as necessary to the expression or the culture of piety as the voice, the look, or the emotions.

It is patent, therefore, that the worship and the lives of the ancient heathens, were based upon cheerful dispositions as well as upon thankful and devout hearts: the gods sang and danced, and their children, following the instructive example, lived—as much as possible, in sweet harmony with the divine institution: ever serene, ever rejoicing both from principle as well as inclination; seeking to be happy in spite of evil; to bask in the full stream of all the sunshine of which our frail nature is susceptible, and which Heaven has kindly ordained for our use to make light, and gay, and contented, the sensitive, ever beating, toiling heart!

The following article in Chambers's Encyclopædia, pertinent to this investigation, will—with few slight omissions: which will—if deemed practicable, be supplied in the sequel, find a welcome notice in the present paragraph: "Dancing," writes the author, "may be defined in a general way as the expression of inward feelings by means of rhythmical movements of the body, especially of the lower limbs, usually accompanied by music. Dancing may almost be said to be as old as the world, and prevails in rude as well as in civilized nations. Children, and also the lower animals, dance and gambol as by instinct. Our early records, sacred and profane, make mention of dancing, and in most of the ancient nations it was a constituent part of their religious rites and ceremonies. They danced before their altars and around the statues of their gods. The Greek *chorus*, " in the oldest times, consisted of the whole population of the city, who met in the public place—*choros*, the market place, to offer up thanksgivings to their countries's god, by singing hymns and performing corresponding dances."

" The Greeks made the art of dancing"—we are further told, " into a system, expressive of all the different passions, the dance of the Eumenides, or Furies, especially, creating such terror, that the spectators seemed to see these dreaded deities about to execute Heaven's vengeance on earth. The most eminent Greek sculptors did not disdain to study the attitudes of the public dancers for their art of imitating the passions. In Homer we read of dancing and music at entertainments. Aristotle ranks dancing with poetry, and says, in his *Poetics*, that there are dancers, who, by rhythm applied to gesture, express manners, passions, and actions. In Pindar, Apollo is called the dancer;* and Jupiter himself—in a Greek line, is represented as in the act of dancing. The Spartans had a law obliging parents to exercise their children in dancing from the age of five. This was done in the public place, to train them for the armed-dance. They were led by grown men, and all sang hymns and songs as they danced. The young men danced the Pyrrhic dance, in four parts, expressive of overtaking an enemy and of a mock-fight.

Nay, dancing, as an entertainment in private society, was performed in ancient times mostly by professional dancers,† and not by the company themselves. Among the sedate Romans, in fact, it was considered disgraceful for a free citizen to dance, *except in connection with religion.* Having professional dancers at entertainments is still the practice among Eastern nations. In Egypt there are dancing and singing girls, called Almé, who improvise verses as in Italy. They are highly educated, and no festival takes place

---

* Apollo and **Pan**—noticed above, often reciprocate personalities.—G.

† **My** knowledge in the matter, clearly makes professional dancers the exceptional instances, as agents in saltatory entertainments. The institution of professional dancers, either in ancient or modern times, except in so far as they *did* or *do* practice the dance as teachers of that charming amusement, is clearly an innovation, while it is a decided improvement in the pristine, saltatory art.—G.

without them. They are placed in rostrums, and
sing during the repast; then descend, and form
dances that have no resemblance to ours. All
over India there are *Nautch girls* or *Bayaderes*,
who dance at festivals and solemnities.

"As a social amusement and a healthful exercise, dancing"—asserts the author in conclusion,
"has much to recommend it; the chief draw-
backs are ill-ventilated and overheated rooms
in which it is generally performed. By many,
it is unfavorably regarded in a moral point of
view; but this seems a relic of that outburst of
puritanism that characterized the seventeenth
century, and which saw sin in every joyous ex-
citement. Dancing is doubtless liable to abuse,
but not more so than most other forms of social
intercourse."

THE DANCES OF THE BIBLE.

CHAPTER I.

The Dances of the Old Testament.

PARAGRAPH I.

Miriam, the Prophetess, Dancing: Exodus, xv. 20–21.

PREFACE.

DANCING, during which songs of praise were sung, formed a very ancient part of the festival solemnities of the Hebrews. After the passage of the Red-Sea, the damsels of Israel, with Miriam at their head, playing on the tabret, sang and danced in celebration of that miraculous event. David himself danced at the induction of the ark into the tabernacle: we learn likewise from the sixty-eighth Psalm, that singers, minstrels, and damsels playing on timbrels, accompanied the sacred processions, and these probably also danced.

62

The yearly festival, held not far from Shiloh, at which the damsels were seized by the Benjamites, consisted of the same amusement. From these authorities, and from the still more explicit terms of the hundred and forty-ninth and the hundred and fiftieth Psalms, we may reasonably maintain that dancing was expressly commanded by the Lord, and it becomes, therefore, the more difficult to understand how certain gloomy censors and narrow-minded theologians can condemn, as sinful, a practice which was distinctly enjoined under the Old Testament, and which is nowhere forbidden by the more recent Gospel. If it was thus prevalent in the public ceremonies and national solemnities of the Hebrews, we cannot doubt that the same recreation, varied by music and singing, constituted one of the principal attractions in their private entertainments, and in the amusements of the domestic circle.*

After the safe and—as we are taught to believe, *miraculous* passage across the Red-Sea, by the Israelites, " Miriam the prophetess, and sister of Aaron, took a timbrel in her hand, and all the women went out after her, with timbrels, and with dancers. And Miriam answered them, Sing ye to the Lord, for he hath triumphed

---

* " Games, Festivals, and Amusements," by Horatio Smith, already noticed on several occasions in this work, and to which the writer thankfully acknowledges his indebtedness.

gloriously: the horse and his rider hath he thrown into the sea."

In his "Oriental Customs," Burder thus comments on the previous passage: "Lady Montague, speaking of the Eastern dances, says their manner is certainly the same as that of the dance of Diana, who—according to mythic lore, was wont to dance on the banks of the Eurotas. The great lady—in Oriental countries, still leads the dance, and is followed by a troop of young girls, who imitate her steps, and, if she sings, make up the chorus. The tunes are extremely gay and lively, yet with something in them wonderfully soft. Their steps are varied according to the pleasure of her that leads the dance, but always in exact time, and infinitely more agreeable than any of our dances."

" This gives us"—continues the author, " a different apprehension of the biblical text, " Miriam the prophetess, the sister of Aaron, *took a timbrel in her hand, and all the women went out after her, with timbrels and dances.* She led the dance, and they imitated her steps, which were not conducted by a set, well-known form, but which were of a purely extemporaneous character."

Here is the sister of two brothers, the one the high-priest, the other the liberator and law-giver of the Jewish nation, seizing a timbrel, and by its sonorous, rhythmic tones, leads in the choral dance, followed by a band of dancers of her own

sex, each—like herself, bearing a timbrel, while
all make merry and all sing devout praises to
Jehovah for the signal deliverance just vouch-
safed to the *Chosen People*, yet we cannot dis-
cover the slightest displeasure manifested by
those distinguished men at this gay, gestic mode
of worship, and must, therefore, infer from their
silence that they considered it acceptable to the
Deity as well as an appropriate and salutary
amusement!

PARAGRAPH II.

The Golden Calf of Aaron the High-Priest, and the Dance-Worship
observed in the Cultus of that Molten Image: Exodus, xxxii. 4th,
5th, 6th, and 19th verses.

The sixth verse in the somewhat ominous heading of the present paragraph, informs us that
the Israelites—as they had been bidden, " rose
up early in the morning; there being, agreeably
to the proclamation of Aaron, the high-priest,
a feast to be celebrated to the Lord on that day,
and, accordingly, having at the appointed time,
brought both burnt-offerings and peace-offerings,
they sat down to eat and to drink—necessary
alimentary acts, which being duly performed,
and, no doubt greatly enjoyed, they finally " rose
up to *play*."

Burder thus pertinently remarks upon the foregoing passage: " It is highly probable that at this
feast the Israelites sacrificed after the manner of

the Egyptians. Thus Herodotus gives an account
of a solemn feast which the people of Egypt celebrated at Bubastis, in honor of the goddess Diana:
to her, he says, they offer many sacrifices, and
while the victim is burning, they *dance*, and play
a hundred tricks, and drink more wine than in
the whole year besides. For they convene thither
to the number of about seven hundred thousand,
both men and women, beside children. Aaron's
feast of the golden calf seems to have been in
imitation of this goddess' feast at Bubastis."*

In the celebration of this great "feast to the
Lord:" it was presumptively of national extent,
dancing, no doubt, formed a conspicuous and
most charming part in the "*play*," and must have

---

* "In the course of the year the Egyptians," writes Herodotus, according to Beloe, "celebrate various public festivals;
but the festival in honor of Diana, in the city Bubastos, is the
first in dignity and importance. The second is held in honor
of Isis, in the city Busiris, which is situated in the middle of
the Delta, and contains the largest temple of that Goddess.
Isis is called in the Greek tongue, Demeter or Ceres. The
solemnities of Minerva, observed in Sais, are the third in
consequence; the fourth are in Heliopolis, and sacred to the
sun; the fifth are those of Latona, in Butos; the next those
of Mars, solemnized in Papremis.

They who meet to celebrate the festival in Bubastos, embark
in vessels a great number of men and women promiscuously
mixed. During the passage, some of the women strike their
tabors, accompanied by men playing on flutes. The rest of
both sexes clap their hands and join in *chorus:* executing
choral dances as a part of the Diana-cultus."

greatly enhanced the interest as well as the impressiveness of the festive rites and dramatic displays of the occasion.

The nineteenth verse referred to in the title of this paragraph, clearly and positively proclaims the fact that dancing—considered as a part of the religious exercises, was observed in honor of the golden calf, and, hence, in so far as this was the case, a perversion from its legitimate use. The text—illustrative of this view, consists in the following pithy and decisive language: " And it came to pass as soon as Moses came nigh unto the camp, that he saw the calf, and the *dancing;* and his anger waxed hot, and he cast the tables out of his hands, and brake them beneath the mount."

This passage does not convey the least intimation that Moses found fault with the dancing of the people on this festive day, but simply with their worship of the golden calf. This further appears from the circumstance, that the golden calf was to be—according to the fourth verse in this connection, a god to the people; for the ingenious founders of idol-images, having finished the *molten* calf, said to the assembled people: " These be thy gods, O Israel, which brought thee up out of the land of Egypt." How *one* golden calf could, under any circumstances, be more than *one* god, it is difficult to conceive and impossible to explain. In the original, the plural is clearly expressed, and the phrase, "these be thy gods," &c., is, therefore, a correct version of the text: commentators may, perhaps, be able to reconcile the palpable discrepancy.

The inquiry demands a brief attention, how the worship of the golden calf could be called "a feast to the Lord." Clearly for the plain reason that it was regarded by the Jews as a symbol or memorial of "the Lord," in conformity with the mythologic customs of antiquity, and that, interpreted in this light, Moses' wrath arose on this remarkable occasion, not on account of the spirit and intention of the worship which was then performed, but because he disapproved of the intervention of any token or reminiscent emblem in the observance of Divine worship.

I will only further add in this connection, that the celebrated golden calf of Aaron, the Jewish high-priest, was primarily no less a being than the Egyptian god *Apis*, the significant and inno- cent symbol anciently of *Taurus or the ox*, simply denoting the path of the sun in that part of the zodiac, indicated in the primitive astronomical calendar by the sign *Taurus*.

Finally, I remark that we have here another proof that the use of the dance in the religious observances of the Jews, was not only *not* disap- proved or censured by the chosen representatives of the Old-Testament theocracy, but evidently cordially sanctioned, and deemed both a prominent and most charming part in the elaborate and gorgeous ritualism of the Jewish Church!

PARAGRAPH III.

A *Feast of the Lord* in Shiloh, and the Daughters of Shiloh *Dancing :* Judges, xxi. 19–21.

" Then they said, " Behold, there is a feast of the Lord in Shiloh yearly in a place, which is on the north side of Bethel, on the east side of the highway that goeth up from Bethel to Shechem, and on the south of Lebonah. Therefore they commanded the children of Benjamin, saying, Go, and lie in wait in the vineyards, and see, and behold, if the daughters of Shiloh come out to *dance in dances*, then come ye out of the vineyards, and catch you every man his wife of the daughters of Shiloh, and go to the land of Benjamin."*

In this interesting and pregnant passage of Sacred Scripture, we notice, first, " a feast of the Lord in Shiloh, and, secondly, " the daughters of

---

* This Benjaminites rape, or violent seizure of " the daughters of Shiloh," has a striking parallel in the famous rape of the Sabine women by the ancient Romans ; men, in both instances, needing wives, and not having enough women for that end of their own, they sought to supply their wants by perfidiously waylaying the fair and unsuspicious daughters of their neighbors. To understand the origin and subsequent incidents, leading to this desperate act of the wife-needy Benjaminites, it is necessary to consult the greater part of the nineteenth, twentieth, and twenty-first chapters of the Book of Judges.

Shiloh dancing in dances." The festival which was celebrated on this cheerful and solemn occasion, was, therefore, both a religious and an anniversary festival: *a feast of the Lord* held in Shiloh *yearly*, in a place adjacent to Bethel. A main accompaniment of the sprightly and yet sacred celebration—it is further to be observed, was the nimble dance: they " danced in dances :" it was indeed, a gay celebration, an emphatically festive rejoicing in the Lord, and quite likely recurred in the spring of the year, when organic nature revives again, and the joys of life unfold themselves clad in new beauty, and glowing in the bright promises of hope.

The substantive for the word *dance* in Hebrew, is *Mahol*, in the singular, and *Maholoth*, in the plural. It invariably signifies a *choral* or round dance—the dancers, while performing it, moving in *chorus*. In its origin it is astronomical, while in its nature it is both symbolical and festive.

The expressive phrase in the text, " they danced in dances," undoubtedly denotes the choral or *Waltz-dances* of the ancients, consisting—as has been stated in a preceding part of this work, " in the strophe, the antistrophe, and the epode :" the three traditionally accepted parts of a normal rotate or ring-dance.

Such being the case, it follows incontestably that the religious dance is not an unacceptable element in the performance of Divine service, nay, that it was, on many occasions, a salient as well as delightful constituent of public worship among the ancient Jews, and that, hence, no protest having been entered against its use either by Jehovah or his authenticated representatives among the Chosen People, who—as the assumed favorites of the Deity, must have known what is most proper in orthodox liturgic observances, I am forced to give to the use of the dance, on appropriate occasions, and in a suitable manner: as virtually a Divinely sanctioned institution, my entire and hearty approval, and I cannot see how any sensible or unprejudiced person can resist or veto this conclusion!

PARAGRAPH IV.

The Women in All the Cities of Israel, are Singing and Dancing: 1 Samuel, xviii. 6–7.

"And it came to pass as they came, when David was returned from the slaughter of the Philistine, that the women came out of all cities of Israel, singing and dancing, to meet King Saul, with tabrets, with joy, and with instruments of music. And the women answered one another as they played, and said, Saul hath slain his thousands, and David his ten thousands."

Burder—the indefatigable explorer of Oriental customs, thus clearly and concisely illustrates the preceding interesting passage: "The dancing, and playing on instruments of music, before persons of distinction, when they pass near the dwelling-places of such as are engaged in country business, still continues in the East. This custom was practiced by some persons in compliment to the Baron Du Tott. He says in his Memoirs: "I took care to cover my escort with my small troop of Europeans; and we continued to march on in this order, which had no very hostile appearance, when we perceived a motion in the enemy's camp, from which several of the Turkomen advanced to meet us: and I soon had the musicians of the different hordes playing and dancing before me, all the time we were passing by the side of their camp." "

The remarkable and wide-spread demonstration: noticed in the text, on the part of an exceedingly numerous body of Jewish women, on this most jubilant and exciting occasion: at once so flattering and encouraging of the national pride, as well as of the feeling of independence and patriotism among the people, was evidently designed to show extraordinary honor in behoof of the distinguished heroes of the Chosen People, Saul and David: especially—it seems, the latter, and to conduct them home in triumph, amid songs, the tabret, and *the dance*. It was—as will readily be perceived, a well-pronounced and splendid *ovation*, indicative mainly of the people' unbounded admiration for the young and gallant conqueror of the warlike and turbulent Philistines.

These sprightly and patriotic women—let us bear in mind, were presumptively members of the Jewish Church, and the fact may, therefore, be reasonably assumed, in a state of grace: owned and blessed by Jehovah. The legitimate and, hence, logical inference is, that what they did in this grand affair of public rejoicing, including *dancing*, as a chief accompaniment of the festive displays on that delightful and memorable event, was at least tacitly approved and publicly recognized as a sacrifice of the heart; replete in *sweet savor ;* acceptable to the Lord; and honorable to man! Then, once more, and once more again,

> " Come and trip it as you go,
> On the light fantastic toe."—MILTON.*

---

* On a certain day, according to Milton—the famous author of " Paradise Lost," God spake to the inhabitants of Heaven, and with his words,

> " All seem'd well pleas'd ; all seem'd, but were not all.
> That day, as other solemn days, they spent
> In song and dance about the sacred hill ;*
> Mystical dance ! which yonder starry sphere
> Of planets and of fix'd stars in all her wheels
> Resembles nearest, mazes intricate,
> Eccentric, intervolv'd, yet regular
> Then most, when most irregular they seem
> And in their motions harmony divine

---

* The Olympus of Heaven !—G.

PARAGRAPH V.

The Induction of the Ark of the Lord, and King David Dancing on
the Joyous Occasion: 2 Samuel, vi. 12th–16th, and 20th verses.

The passage in which the glory of the dance
in the Jewish ritual exercises, attains its culmi-
nation, is, no doubt, that which forms the subject
of the present paragraph, and of which the reader
will find a notice in its appropriate place. Its
prolific import is thus succinctly set forth : " And
it was told king David, saying, The Lord hath
blessed the house of Obed-edom, and all that
pertaineth unto him, because of the ark of God.
So David went and brought up the ark of God
from the house of Obed-edom into the city of
David with gladness. And it was so, that when
they that bare the ark of the Lord had gone
six paces, he sacrificed oxen and fatlings. And
David *danced before the Lord with all his might;*
and David was girded with a linen ephod. So
David and all the house of Israel brought up
the ark of the Lord with shouting, and with the
sound of the trumpet. And as the ark of the

　　So smooths her charming tones, that God's own ear
　　Listens delighted."*

Such was, in brief, Milton's estimation of the dance.
Heaven's pure and holy joys could not be solemnized without the angelic waltz or round-dance—symbolic of planetary
motion, when *God's own ear listened delighted !*

* Book V., p. 118, 2⅔.

Lord came into the city of David, Michal, Saul's daughter, looked through a window, and saw king David *leaping* and *dancing* before the Lord; and she despised him in her heart. And Michal, the daughter of Saul, came out to meet David, and said, How glorious was the king of Israel to-day, who uncovered himself to-day in the eyes of the handmaids of his servants, as one of the vain fellows shamelessly uncovereth himself!"

Here again, we find the dance—saltant child of Terpsichore, employed as a pleasant and, indeed, powerful adjunct of the festive rites of the Jews; nay, judging from the general tenor of the Old Testament on this engrossing subject, the dance may without exaggeration, I think, be defined as a prominent and leading part of the religious exercises of the Chosen People, in the earlier and more pastoral eras of their civil polity and ecclesiastical integrity.

But if this statement conveys a true idea of the nature and the tendencies of the dance, why was Michal " the daughter of Saul," and the wife of David, so grievously mortified on account of the king's dancing on this jubilant event, when the thought of the restoration of the long-absent ark of God, filled all hearts with gladness, while it appeared as the hallowed pledge of a brighter future? Why, moreover, does she taunt him by mockingly saying, " How glorious was the king of Israel to-day!"

The reason is patent: the king, in the exuberance of his great joy in at last being able to induct the ark of the Lord to Jerusalem: *his own city*, indulged—it must be admitted, in rather extravagant and somewhat uncouth *leaps* in the delight of his devout soul, during his saltatory exhibitions, and what must be regarded as still more reprehensible in his jocund, orchestic performances, was the immodest behavior with which Michal, no doubt, justly charged her lord, who—she said, like "one of the vain fellows, shamelessly uncovered himself in the presence of his hand-maids." Thus, as was much to be feared, and as Michal especially must have apprehended, inevitably lowering his kingly dignity in the eyes of his subjects as well as losing the respect and willing homage of the members of his royal household.

Michal does not utter even a single syllable in condemnation of the dance, as a mere amusement, or an element in ritual observances, but wisely confines her strictures to his abuse, and the grave evils which must result from an imprudent or vicious indulgence of the dance, considered either in its relation to divine worship, or simply as an appropriate means of a rational and healthful pastime: the moral sense of the nineteenth century will not hesitate to approve the censure and applaud the courage of this eminently considerate and sober-minded Hebrew matron.

If now we call to mind, that David, who is said in the text, to "have danced before the Lord with all his might," was "the sweet Psalmist of Israel;" that, in numerous places of the Old Testament, he is described and extolled as the nationally recognized *pattern*-man and king: as even " the man after God's own heart;" that one, like him, was the ever anticipated, ever sought, great deliverer, and sure as well as speedy avenger of the often oppressed and distracted Jewish nation, in those sad and calamitous times that " tried men's souls"—in short, a mighty friend and resistless conqueror, hailed as the venerable and resplendent scion of the house of David; and that, finally, the genealogy of Jesus Christ himself, the Saviour, is—*according to the flesh*, traced to the lofty lineage of David, the king and devout lyrist of Israel, we must conclude that when he danced, whether the occasion was secular or religious, he danced like " a man having authority" for what he did, and, hence, exemplifying and vindicating a custom, which must—being thus unmistakably authenticated, have, at once, the character and the force of a Divine institution. Therefore, in taking leave of the present disquisition, I say, in the significant and impressive language of Gay :

" Seek virtue ; and of that possess'd,
To Providence resign the rest."

PARAGRAPH VI.

The Dance—a Means of Consolation: Psalm, xxx. 11.

One of the most extraordinary opinions, ever advanced in the Bible, is certainly that which is contained in the eleventh verse of the thirtieth Psalm. In this lyric effusion of sentiment and genius of a remote age, the writer—ostensibly David, says: " *Thou* hast turned for me my mourning *into dancing: thou* has put off my sackcloth, and girded me with gladness."

What, we are in deep mourning, and to be comforted, or to be delivered from this sad and depressing state of the soul, we need but resort to the use of the nimble, sprightly dance, and, at once, our sackcloth is cast off, while gladness, like a magic band, girds up the wounded heart, and, behold, it is whole!

What, however, is the most remarkable circumstance in this great and wonderful psychological cure, is that—according to the plain, positive statement in the text, *God himself* turned the mourning of the Psalmist into *dancing!* What astounding doctrine this is! Can it possibly be sound and of redeeming efficacy; nay, can it be promotive of even the simplest, feeblest ethical principles? Did Luther, or Calvin, Anslem, or St. Augustin ever teach anything akin to such strange and incredible novelties? How then can the Psalmist be orthodox, or the Bible be any longer worthy of faith and confidence ?

I am really apprehensive that should this decidedly heterodox teaching of the Psalmist come to the knowledge of some of our *true believers*, according to the usually accepted canons of orthodoxy, the Psalmist would, no doubt, fare badly, for nothing would, most likely, satisfy them, should they have the power as well as the will, but the use of the purifying and saving flames of an *auto da fe!*

Nevertheless, let us hope, and, if necessary, pray, that the result, in any event, will not assume so disastrous a character, and that the common-sense example of reasonable people, will not only be the means of vindicating the Psalmist's strange teaching, but prove instrumental in furtherance of praises and thanks-givings to God, for graciously " turning our mourning *into dancing !*"

PARAGRAPH VII.

The Dance is a Means of Praising God: Psalms, cxlix. 3 ; cl. 4.

The first Scripture-passage, pointed out in the title of this paragraph, exhorts Israel " to praise the name of the Lord, *in the dance :*" " let them"—continues the exhortation, " sing praises unto him with the timbrel and the harp."

The second passage, qualified by the same prefix, and referred to, under this head, is substantially the same as the preceding, and is thus expressed: "Praise God with the timbrel and dance: praise him with stringed instruments and organs."*

In the religious practices of the *Shakers* and *the Jumpers*—two very euphonic titles, we have contemporary examples of the important part, which the dance performs in the routine of religious service. I regret to say, however, that the use which these sects seem to make of this means, so admirably adapted to express the joyous sentiments of devotion, is—if we can rely upon the information of Buck's "Theological Dictionary," relatively to this subject, extravagant, uncouth, and often offensive to good taste as well as incompatible with strictly good morals.

The abuse of the dance, in the worship of God, is, however, by no means a sufficient reason why it should not be *properly* used, in devotional exercises. Nor can it, in the least, invalidate the force and relevancy of the exhortations of the writers of the salient texts, submitted to this brief review. If modern religionists thoughtlessly infringe upon the rightful use of a Divine and valuable institu-

---

* The erudite De Wette, in his "Commentar über die Psalmen," translates the Hebrew nouns, rendered *dance*, in the English version, by the phrase *Reigen*, which denotes a *choral* or round-dance, and which was, therefore, performed by a *chorus*, more or less in the style of a Waltz: the symbol —as has already been stated, of *planetary motion.*

tion, eminently pertinent in the devout and joyful expressions of thanks and praises to God, it does not logically follow or necessarily involve the issue, that the Psalmists' teaching of Israel, " To praise the name of the Lord in the dance; yea, to praise him with the timbrel and the dance," should not be earnestly heeded, and diligently as well as faithfully carried out.

It is generally deemed to be exceedingly proper, and strictly conformably to nature and the wants of the occasion, when we are borne down with sorrow, or oppressed by want, to seek the succor and the consolations of religion, and—at such lugubrious and trying times, to wear a becoming air of sadness and humility, corresponding to the desolation of the stricken heart within, and why should we not assume a corresponding demeanor, and manifest a responsive behavior—when we are animated with cheerful thoughts; when the events and circumstances in our lives, conspire to make glad the soul, and it is natural and salutary to indulge in the graceful attitudes of the measured steps, and the sprightly inflections of the mirthful passions?

To be sedate and gloomy in the youthful period of our lives, shows a morbid state of the mind, and is clearly an exceptional manifestation of normal human nature. The same unsound or *abnormal* state of mind, is witnessed in that portion of mankind, who abound in the possession of choice blessings, and are invited by every pleasing incident in nature; by every glow or emotion of pleasure, to rejoice in the goodness of God, and who, nevertheless—owing to false shame or a depraved imagination, foolishly suppress those sentiments, which it is entirely proper as well as natural, to indulge, on all suitable occasions, in the delightful practice of music and *the dance:* twin-arts of birth-divine, sent to make glad the heart of man!

PARAGRAPH VIII.

There is a Time to Dance: Ecclesiastes, iii. 4.

" There is a time to dance," says the Preacher. —This text, though brief, and therefore easily legible, is of decidedly pithy import: it is an example of those salient expressions, which pass under the significant denomination, familiarly known as *proverbs*, and which are chiefly synonymous with the phrase, *wise sayings.* Who is the author of it, is not certainly known. Nor does it matter a great deal, as the book in which it occurs, has *a canonical* reputation, and is, therefore, it should seem, of Divine authority!

The book—as the heading of this paragraph shows, is called *Ecclesiastes*, a name which means preacher: a very vague designation, and which decides positively nothing as to its authorship. Until more recent times, it has generally been attributed to the learned pen of King Solomon, but the fallacy of such an opinion, is now apparent among most biblical scholars, and hence its claims to a regal pedigree, are no longer admissible.

The proposition, There is a time to dance, had so long been considered so very wise a saying, that at length the presumption began to be entertained, that only a man like Solomon—*the wise Solomon!** could have been the writer of it together with the other pregnant and interesting literature, contained in Ecclesiastes. There are doctrines advanced in this eminently instructive though somewhat skeptical work, which evince far more wisdom than ever Solomon displayed in the administration of his little and obscure kingdom; for the brief and pointed sentence, " There is a time to dance," clearly implies much more sober wisdom and chaste sentiment, than the ridiculous maintenance of a harem, composed of the modest and exemplary number of " *seven hundred wives, and three hundred concubines!*"

That there is a time to dance, we are expressly informed, but the meaning cannot be that *every* person is to dance; or that a time is allotted by Providence to every person, in which he must absolutely dance; for all persons are not capable of dancing, either on account of bodily infirmities;

---

* " Lo," says God, according to First Kings, third chapter and twelfth verse, " I have given thee a wise and an understanding heart, so that there was none like thee before thee, neither after thee shall any arise like unto thee."

want of inclination; or, finally, want of a proper vivacity and cheerfulness of spirits.

The unqualified assertion, therefore, that there is a time to dance—a time in every person's life, when he must deem it a duty as well as a pleasure, to dance, can only be strictly applicable to him, who has the requisite qualifications and inducements to dance, and he will not need to be exhorted to indulge in the sprightly, saltant pastime: he will dance spontaneously, impulsively, and irresistibly—unless restraint by the rules of art, or checked by conventional prescription, just as certainly and naturally as he will eat or talk, rest or think!

By the statement of the proverb, which forms the theme of this investigation, that there is a time to dance, it is to be taken for granted that reference is virtually made to the religious as well as to the secular dance: to the dance, devoted to recreation, health, refinement, and to the dance, sacred to liturgic rites; for the writer of that pregnant saying was, no doubt, a *Jew*, and the Chosen People were perfectly familiar—as has already been demonstrated, with the sprightly Terpsichorean muse—lovely queen of the dance, in both regards.

It is, indeed, difficult to see and impossible to understand, why man cannot just as devoutly and acceptably manifest his reverence and devotion towards the Almighty, with his feet as with his tongue, hands or his looks! Are not all the human organs and motions alike the workmanship of the Divine hands, and alike good and praiseworthy in themselves? What is the difference— in a moral point of view, whether I sing or dance, or pray, smile or scowl, in the name and to the glory of the Lord? All that is really required, in all modes and forms of religious services, is, "that everything"—according to St. Paul, "should be done *decently and in order.*" The Hebrews—members of the Old-Testament Church, habitually and approvingly worshipped God in the dance, and why should it not be proper to introduce the dance into the Christian Church, as a leading and holy element in the cultus of the New Testament? *Unto the pure all things are pure!*—Titus, first chapter and fifteenth verse.

PARAGRAPH IX.

What Jeremiah says in Reference to the Dance, in his Prophecies, xxxi. 4, 11–13; what he says on the Same Subject, in his Lamentations, v. 15.

In the prophetic portions of the book of Jeremiah, noticed in the title of this article, the dance is represented as the necessary and irrevocably God-ordained sequence of the felicitous and encouraging turn, which the gloomy and distressing calamities of the Jews, considered in their national capacity, had taken, or should take at some future time, as a token and pledge—according to the Prophet, of the goodness of God, who had graciously resolved so to order the course of Divine providence, as to render the events in the social polity and religious experience of his people, a source of profound rejoicing amid the harmonic chords of music, and the happy, jocund *dance!*

As the interesting and terse teachings of the Prophet on this subject, in the thirty-first chapter of his copious Prophecies, are strictly and pleasingly concordant with the thesis laid down in the thirtieth Psalm, already elucidated and maturely treated in these pages, further comment here is deemed superfluous.

In the passage of the *Lamentations* of the Prophet —as set forth in the Scripture-references of the present paragraph, the dance has, alas! ceased, as an evidence and necessary result of the calamitous and mournful visitations of the unfortunate Jewish nation, which naturally express themselves in plaintive tones and pitiful lamentation. Whenever— we are taught here, in this Hebrew branch, among the descendants of Shem, reverses of fortune brought misery and suffering in their disastrous train, mourning, sighs, and tears gushed forth as the natural and irrepressible elements in their sad and painful destiny: they were, indeed, the direful and chastening *insignia* of a prostrate and humbled condition of the Chosen People, and to have then rejoiced, or indulged in jolliness, in lively music,

or *the light, fantastic* dance, would have been a
flagrant and grossly sinful violation of the innate,
and, therefore, natural sentiments of the human
heart : " to everything there is a season ;" yes, " a
time to mourn, and a time to dance !"

It is possible that in the foregoing researches
on the subject of the dance, some matter relevant
to this interesting branch of human knowledge,
has eluded the writer's grasp, should such be the
case, it behooves him to say that nothing which is
essential to the subject—to make the investigation literally exhaustive, and, therefore, it is to be
hoped satisfactory, has escaped his careful scrutiny.

The notice of the dance, as a prominent and
vigorous element in the social life of the Hebrews,
is thus concluded : " If an exercise so sociable and
enlivening," writes Rev. Fordyce, in his " Sermons
to Young Persons," " were to occupy some part
of that time which is lavished on cards, would the
youth of either sex be losers by it ? I think not.
It seems to me there can be no impropriety in it,
any more than in modulating the voice into the
most agreeable tones in singing, to which none,
I think, will object. What is dancing, in the most
rigid sense, but the harmony of motion rendered
more palpable ? Awkwardness, rusticity, ungrace-
ful gestures, can never surely be meritorious."*

---

* Smith : Festivals, Games, and Amusements.

CHAPTER II.

PARAGRAPH I.

Dancing was a Common Practice among the Jews, in the Time of the Savior, and passed unrebuked by the *Son of Man :* Matthew, xi. 16–17.

THE following are the salient no less than forcible words, to which the simple and concise heading of this paragraph refers : " But whereunto," says Christ, "shall I liken this generation? . It is like unto children sitting in the markets, and calling unto their fellows, and saying, We have piped unto you, and ye have not danced; we have mourned unto you, and ye have not lamented."

Here the interesting and pleasing fact is prominently brought to light, that *dancing*—the grand and delightful Terpsichorean art, was so common and highly esteemed among the Jews in the Savior's time, that it ranked among the usual plays or pastimes of their children. These juvenile representatives of the Hebrew race,. had the sportive and sociable habit of meeting in the markets, or—as Doctor Clarke very properly suggests, other public places of resort, where it was customary for the ingenious and pleasure-seeking

88

lads to entertain each other with the music of the
favorite pipe, and the rhythmic evolutions, or
rather, perhaps, the impulsive *ejaculations* of the
dance.

So common and admired, it seems, was this
charming orchestic amusement in Judæa, that if
the loved dance did not immediately respond to
the emphatic melody of the pipe, the omission
created great astonishment as well as disappointment, and the complaint was made, in tones of
deeply injured feelings, indicative of implied reproach: " We have piped unto you, and ye would
not dance !"

The Savior here indirectly censures the listless
and obdurate Jews, who were alike indifferent to
the joyful or the humiliating visitations of Divine
providence : he might endeavor to approach them
in any of the avenues by which the human heart
is generally accessible, and his humane efforts
were, alas, mainly futile !   But he does not even
in the slightest degree insinuate disapprobation
or condemnation of the common and—as it appears from the tenor of the text, widely prevalent practice of dancing, among his countrymen,
reasonably and truthfully entertaining the idea—
as was most likely under the circumstances of the
case, and as Doctor Clarke remarks in his exegesis on this significant passage, that " everything
is good to an upright mind, everything bad to a
vicious heart" !

PARAGRAPH II.

Dancing in High Life: Matthew, xiv. 6-8.

The text, which serves as a basis of this article, and which is here accordingly indicated in the heading, contains words of grave import, well-calculated to lead to profound reflection. A closer inquiry will find it briefly thus stated: "But when Herod's birth-day was kept, the daughter of Herodias danced before them, and pleased Herod. Whereupon he promised with an oath to give her whatsoever she would ask. And she, being before instructed of her mother, said, Give me here John Baptist's head in a charger."

The festive celebration of birth-days, reaches far back in the incipient annals of time, and, in the striking narrative before us, we have a distinguished instance of a recurrence of such an event, eighteen centuries ago, within the ample walls of a splendid and luxurious palace in the renowned land of Judæa.

The person, in whose honor this gorgeous natal festival was observed, was no less a man than Herod Antipas, tetrarch of Galilee and Perea, bearing the title *king*, as is evident from the ninth verse of this birth-day drama. This petty ruler, whose habits, it appears, were more profligate than chaste, lived in illicit intercourse with Herodias, the wife of his brother Philip, who was still living, and with whom she had a daughter, named Salome—the cynosure of the present festivity, and—of course, the niece of the uxorious Herod Antipas.

Salome—as we learn from the lucid narrative of this gay and imposing commemorative fête, at which she appeared *in the part of solo-dancer*, was an accomplished performer in the mysteries and graces of the elegant and attractive art of the Terpsichorean muse, and, in giving proof before her royal uncle, of the exquisite skill to which she had attained in its elegant graces, he was delighted to such a degree, that — in a transport of munificence, he forgot the princely virtues of justice and humanity, and "promised with an oath to give her whatsoever she would ask."

Instigated by her libidinous mother, whose proud and revengeful disposition stood out in bold relief on this joyous yet tragic occasion, she unthinkingly as well as, most likely, unconscious of evil, "asked John Baptist's head in a charger," and her prayer—which was granted, though with reluctance, caused *sorrow* to the king, and the loss of the head of the blunt and honest " Forerunner of Christ"!

It is clear that, however criminal the conduct of the royal couple may have been in the commission of the dark and cruel deed, perpetrated on this hilarious and reminiscent pastime, the admirable dancer, Salome, performed but a very inferior rôle in the bloody scene. The part which she took in it, was that of an instrument in the hands of her mother, and her free-agency was really never called into requisition. She may have been an indiscreet, giddy young lady, moved by impulse rather than reason, but she cannot be justly charged with *conscious intent* of doing an evil deed, or—with predilection for evil, commit a wrong.

As to the relation of the dance to the death of the Baptist, that was decidedly *accidental*, and can hence cast no injurious reflection on that pleasing and useful saltant art or recreative amusement. Nor does the Scripture, Christ or any Apostle, in this place or elsewhere, speak disapprovingly of the dance, or denounce it as instrumental of evil, on account of this lamentable affair, or any similar untoward incident in human experience. At any rate, the dance and the dancer must not be confounded; no, no more than God and the incidental evils resulting from his works, of which he has peremptorily affirmed in the first chapter of the book of Genesis, That, " *they are very good*" ! I add that, in taking leave of Salome, the fair, Jewish dancer, we will not also take leave of the dance, contemplated as an eminently agreeable and useful art, but with Byron still say with unwearied assiduity:

" On with the dance ! let joy be unconfined !"

PARAGRAPH III.

The Dance and the Prodigal Son: Luke, xv. 25.

" Now his elder son was in the field, and as he came and drew nigh to the house, he heard music and dancing," such is the weighty and significant import of the text, pointed out in the concise title of this paragraph, and replete with pregnant and instructive information, as well as largely suggestive of the urgent need of change in our generally received dogmas of God and heaven.

In the following comments and quotation, Burder throws valuable light upon the subject of the present inquiry: " To express the joy which the return of the prodigal afforded his father, *music and dancing* were provided as a part of the entertainment. This expression does not however denote the dancing of the family and guests, but that of a company of persons hired on this occasion for that very purpose. Such a practice prevailed in some places to express peculiar honor to a friend, or joy upon any special occasion.

Major Rooke, in his travels from India through Arabia Felix, relates an occurrence which will illustrate this part of the parable: " Hadje Cassim, who is a Turk, and one of the richest merchants in Cairo, had interceded on my behalf with Ibrahim Bey, at the instance of his son,

who had been on a pilgrimage to Mecca, and
came from Judda in the same ship with me.
The father, in celebration of his son's return,
gave a most magnificent fete on the evening of
the day of my captivity, and as soon as I was re-
leased, sent to invite me to partake of it, and I
accordingly went. His company was very numerous, consisting of three or four hundred
Turks, who were all sitting on sophas and
benches, smoking their long pipes. The room
in which they were assembled, was a spacious
and lofty hall, in the center of which was a band
of music, composed of five Turkish instruments,
and some vocal performers : as there were no
ladies in the assembly, you may suppose it was
not the most lively party in the world, but
being new to me, was for that reason entertaining." "

The two sons, mentioned in the parable, now
demand a brief attention. Who are they? The
sons of "a certain man." In what relation—it
may be desirable to know, do they stand to each
other in respect to age? I answer, in the relation of sequence: the one son is, hence, called
" the elder," the other, " the younger."

Next we must endeavor to attain to a correct
knowledge of character of each of the brothers,
and then to form an impartial judgment of their
virtues or vices. The task, I think, will be easy,
and the result appreciated; for the *parable* that

gives rise to the problem, also supplies the means
of its solution.

Soon after the younger son had received "the
portion of goods," which he claimed of his father,
he left home, and ere long " wasted his substance
with riotous living," or—in the energetic language of his brother, " he devoured his father's
living with harlots"! The elder son led a very
different life; for says he, " Lo, these many years
do I serve thee, neither transgressed I, at any
time, thy commandment!" Hence the elder son
may be said to have been a person, who observed
a regular life, and was, therefore, *a moral man;*
the younger son, a person, whose life was the
opposite of this, and who was, hence, an immoral
or wicked man! I will only add that the for-
mer's mode of life was evidently approved by the
father, in spite of the contemners of good works,
as means of acceptance with God, while the latter's vicious career could only be expiated by
hearty repentance!

Our further inquiry is, who was the *father*, to
whom these morally diverse sons traced their
parentage? A man—a wealthy man, perhaps a
powerful prince, but only a man, say most commentators. The reasons for such a conclusion,
seem to be based upon considerations like the
following: The father having ordered " a fatted
calf" to be killed, said, "let *us eat and be merry,*" &c.

Besides, there is, among other modes of joy-

ous demonstrations, on the happy occasion of
the prodigal's return, also that of *dancing* in the
father's *house*. A house thus designated, it is
taught, must signify an earthly father's house,
for in the "Father's house" *with many mansions*,
there is *no dancing*. The sequel will show whether
this opinion, so dogmatically expressed, should
not at least be held a little longer in abeyance!

When Lazarus died—according to the sixteenth
chapter of the Gospel of St. John, "he was carried
by angels into Abraham's bosom." Exegetes are
unanimous in the opinion that this phraseology
denotes a *banquet-scene*, and, hence, there must be
not only eating or partaking of material food in
heaven, but there must be likewise *tricliniaries*,
there, that is, "couches for dining, according to
the ancient mode of reclining at table," as Webster—according to antiquarian teaching, pertinently remarks. Now if such sensuous, material
habits of life as are common on earth, are still
perpetuated in heaven, why should it be deemed
a desecration to indulge there in the *dance?*

In addition to the foregoing facts, the twenty-
second chapter of St. Matthew, too furnishes
proof, that the *father* in the parable, is not a
human father, but a Divine father, nay, *God himself*. Here—as stated by Jesus, "A certain king,"
made a marriage-feast for his son, and when he
came in to see the guests, one of them had not
on "a wedding-garment," and he was summarily

cast out. Now what can be meant by this marriage-feast but the Christian Church: synonymous with "Kingdom of Heaven," first, and immediately, in its militant relations; secondly, and remotely, in its triumphant and supernatural state? Hence I feel warranted in the inference, that by the expression, "A certain king," Jesus means *God,* and by the place where the distinguished guests were assembled, *Heaven!*

I shall here advert to but one more source, strongly suggestive of the probable accompaniment of the dance among the hallowed and ecstatic joys of the heavenly state : that source is "the New Jerusalem," described in the twenty-first and the twenty-second chapters of the Apocalypse, and which the writer of that allegorical and somewhat mystic production, says "was coming down from God out of heaven." The appurtenances, distinguishing it, are fully of as material and earthly a nature as the dance; as, for example, we find in it a river, a wall, gates, fountains, precious stones, yet essentially only stones, streets, a throne, a tree of life, bearing twelve kinds of fruit, and yet God is in this "holy city"—the heaven of many of the early Christians, as is emphatically stated in the third verse of the twenty-first chapter : " And I heard a great voice out of heaven"—thus asserts the author, " saying, Behold, the tabernacle of God is with men, and he will dwell with them, and they shall be his

people, and God himself shall be with them, and
be their God!"

THE CONCLUSION.

There is no reason then, on the score of propriety, why *dancing* should not rank among the
paradisiacal elements of happiness in heaven, and
why the *house*, mentioned in the parable, was not
meant to denote that felicitous abode.   I believe
it was, and I also believe that *the father*, used in
connection with the narrative of "the prodigal
son," most unequivocally and according to sound
exegesis, means God!

Where is heaven?   Is it not everywhere? and
is not, therefore, God, who is—as we are taught,
in heaven, everywhere?   Hence, we may conclude
that a great many worse and less seemly deeds
than are implied in dancing, are done in his august
and holy presence—in his "house of many mansions"!   I add, in the pithy words of Sidney,
while I bid a long and affectionate farewell to
sweet, graceful Terpsichore :

"The love of heaven makes one heavenly!"

THE END.